Viscera

Also by Angela Carole Brown

Trading Fours, 2005

The Assassination of Gabriel Champion, 2013

The Kidney Journals: Memoirs of a Desperate Lifesaver, 2014

Aleatory on the Radio, 2019

Bones, 2019

Viscera

Angela Carole Brown

HAIKU HOUSE

Viscera

Copyright @ 2019 by Angela Carole Brown

Cover art by Paulina Franco
Graphic design and layout by Angela Carole Brown
Photo of Angela and Hans San Juan by Annamarie Rewal

Published by Haiku House
First Edition
ISBN-13: 978-1-7337453-2-1

Preface

On July 22, 2008, at Cedars-Sinai Medical Center in Los Angeles, California, I donated a kidney to teenager Hans San Juan, to whom I was connected through his parents, who are my dear friends. The transplant was considered a success, and over the next ten years an abiding friendship/familyship was forged. During that decade, Hans grew up, got married, made music, and lived his full, rich life.

At the 10-year mark, the kidney failed, and Hans went back on dialysis. As his loved ones began the long, arduous campaign for a second transplant and finding another donor, this suite of poems came into being; a primal scream, a rallying cry. Hungry, angry, hangry, slaphappy.

In determining what I wanted for the book's cover, I decided that the perfect person to create it, who would be emotionally invested in this, would be Hans' young wife, a beautiful artist named Paulina Franco. We had a conversation, and I asked her to create an image of Hans; abstract or realism, whatever called out to her; all I knew was that I wanted him bearing wings. Ever the championing wife, Paulina rejected the idea of angel's wings, as she refused to envision Hans as no longer here. I loved her indignations. When I clarified that butterfly or dragonfly wings were more along the lines of my thinking, she quickly jumped on the butterfly wings, which we both decided perfectly symbolized the metamorphosis Hans was continually undergoing in his pursuit of health and happiness. And a portrait was born.

Memoir in narrative verse, *Viscera* riffs on survival and the inexplicable life force of the young.

Angela Carole Brown

Los Angeles, 2019

Contents

keep him in gentle accord

Deadly Nightshade

The beast took his run tonight.

Scampered across a black moorland that erupted in belladonna

& willowherbs, interspersed with trees

that stood like soldiers at attention.

He stopped suddenly in front of me, amber eyes hooking mine,

reeling me in like a Trinity River catch in summer.

This beast, a shadow of indeterminate form, visits my dreams frequently.

Comes to me like a neuron firing, or a floater in the corner of my eye.

Just an instant of something passing. Did I really see something?

Until he hooks me. Burrows into the cells of my pain.

Forewarns of tests that await me, gentle in spirit & delivery.

I call him beast in order to retain the myths of good & evil.

In order to insure my place on the right side. Yet his eyes are tender.

I stare into them until I fall deeply inside, wading around in the viscera.

Until I hear his howls, a weeping falsetto, bending notes to his will.

Until I can bend my voice with his. Until. Until. Until we are a duet.

God Shot

The trending term these days in the
spiritual, new age, blah blah
movement is *god shot*.
I would imagine it's not meant to conjure
random stabbings that take one to
the ground only to yank 'em back up
by the nape and throw a halo on that head,
or a smackhead's desperate inoculation,
needle to vein in an ecstatic dance,
only instead of it being followed by
the nod-&-stupor, or the dirty blood
beading and stippling, the result
is a halo thrown on that head.
I would imagine not. But that's
what it does. No matter how I picture it,
the image always feels violent *and* invigorating.

A kidney for Hans would be called a god shot.
The most invigorating event of my life.
His too, I dare say. But violent?
A kidney severed from one tissue-&-blood
supply to be inserted and sewn into
another seems pretty violent to me.

See, so, violence isn't always bad.
Or maybe I'm just in a mood because
here we are 10 years later, and he is
back where he started, transplanted
kidney suddenly feeling the bang of a
head-on. And just the word "shot," man.
It's not a gentle word. It has power.
A god shot can't be gentle. It must be
infused with a jolt, a nosedive,
an unapologetic concussion.
It has to be startling. Off-putting even.
Because nothing graced can be tepid.

The phone call from Cedars that I was
a match and would, barring my own
cowardice, be this 19-year-old's donor
was a god shot. That's easy.
Waking up from surgery, and hearing
through the Dilaudid fog that all
procedures had gone well, a god shot.
EASY. Ten glorious years of the relocated
kidney working, pumping, filtering, keeping
him alive, a damned god shot. It revs

the metabolism thinking about it. But
here's where it gets testy. Or I get testy.

Is this new twist — transplanted kidney
starting its fail, a saturated bloat of toxic
fluids resculpting my boy (a man now) into
someone else, the word finally in: *It's been
a good 10 years, but the kidney is done* —
also a god shot?

Because if you believe in god shots, then
you believe in god shots. *But—*
No ma'am! If you believe in god shots,
then you believe in god shots.
This Religion of Coddling's jig is up.
If you're naming it, then you're
naming it. No salves. No unguents for
fragile souls.
Embrace your darkest hours, your deepest waters,
your surest of curses, as the blessings they actually are.
Every toxic pore, inflamed capillary,
and clogged glomerular honeycomb is
drenched in grace, even huffing and puffing,

even collapsing beneath the muddy boot of treachery.

Even blackened with necrosis and smelling like offal.

What doesn't kill you...

If I can only let go.

If I can only let go, I know I can shift the earth's plates,

make them bend to my will.

Breathe the freaking life back into this bitch.

Kidney failure, you bitch!

Take my breath, my boy, and breathe.

Just breathe. Let us breathe in concert.

1-2-3. 2-2-3. 3-2-3. A waltz is the

most tangible rhythm to assist breathing.

Let us glide, dancing into the fathoms to

some furious Strauss or other, soaking

in the ancient oaks and hieroglyphs,

foraging for food like rabid dogs.

Let us shoot the poisoned arrow of God into the

spleen of misfortune and birth defects, and

laugh Death in the face with our precision shot.

Let us claim the spoils.

i did not do this for you

this was not selfless

Afraid

I never wanted to be a parent. Never had

the pull. But I birthed you. Nine months of testing

later, you emerged new. Your mother is

kind enough to allow me room to do this,

play with this, as if it is a toy, as if

you are a toy.

The afterbirth I've lapped up

has kept me fed all these years.

Now I wonder who'll become your next donor,

who'll take my place and perhaps your heart.

It is the most selfish thought I could possibly think.

I did not do this for you. This was not selfless.

I was drowning. Downed to the swamp's mossy depths.

I needed the epi shot.

I never wanted to be a parent. Now my

heart hurts like glass, tacky as glue,

and I am stuck on flypaper,

trying to pry myself from hubris.

Afraid to lose you to death.

Afraid to lose you to another lifegiver.

Afraid to lose my soul in this thought.

Afraid I already have.

¡Sangre! ¡Ahora!

He is obsessed with Gustavo Dudamel.

Could be found routinely in the seats

in the early years of the conductor's

L.A. reign. Got to watch a rehearsal once.

The maestro was frustrated, fixated on a

section that simply was not working to his

satisfaction. Kept shouting, "Where is the

blood?" Over and over, "Where is the

blood?" When finally something began

to take shape worthy of the music,

Dudamel exclaimed passionately, accent

dripping like Chocolates La Colonia,

" N o w   w e   h a v e   b l o o d ! "

This Hans seized upon.

Blood Hans gets.

The taste of metals upon the lips.

Flesh kneaded, prodded and bruised

into submission, as the pudding beneath

the surface forms. Veins drained and

refreshed daily like the miraculous,

vampiric pinking of the dead.

A corporeal wonderland

stained with promise.

Using the maestro's

zealous proclamation

for its title,

Hans ran home that day

and composed an entire

album of music.

Blood is his first language.

His urgent vow.

Inheritance

He was singing a song I
wrote when he awakened

from the anesthesia (or so
the family legend tells it).

He claimed to be suddenly
having menopausal mood

swings and hot flashes.
This 19-year-old kid.

We've laughed a lot over
this. Though secretly I've

worried that what he'd
really inherit would be

my anxieties, my penchant
for self-immolation and

moroseness. Be suddenly

saddled with compulsive

behaviors born from a

childhood of outcastness

that raped the double helix a

full generation before he was

even given to this earth. Would

he wrestle in the night hours

with his place in the world?

Or fly in spite of me?

make me the bludgeon to comfort and plans

Preying

Alan Watts

taught me that

everything

is flux.

Motherhood

has said,

Hell to the damn no, sir!

and yanks on this

childless womb

with an unceasing,

frozen grip,

while I channel

Shirley MacLaine with,

"SOMEBODY GIVE MY BOY A KIDNEEEEEY!"

I pounce like a cat every day on Facebook

these days. Let the claws protrude from

their cozy, and gently scrape

everyone's nape with the

promise of something deeper,

blood-drawing, if somebody doesn't…

what? step forward? bow to my ornery will?

I scroll past every event I see —

"Jerry is raising money for..." or "Tarika is donating to..." —

without giving a single one of them a moment of my time.

Who am I to jut my neck

when all I get are some likes,

a few appreciated shares, but not much else?

A recent post of mine:

He needs another kidney, folks.

And I'm all out. Who's willing?

It ain't scary. It's grace.

Then I quote Gandhi,

but with a not-even-remotely-Gandhi eye roll.

I am the

mothering-

fucking

brigade.

That is, until 2 days in

5 days in

3 weeks in,

when I am more

scattered showers than

predatory squall.

Dear God don't let me

drift away from this.

Don't let me go back to

being the girl whose tire

never touches the white line

on a snaking road in order

to straighten out her drive.

Make me the bludgeon

to comfort and plans,

preying unrelenting,

till a new hope

comes forward

to knock it

out of the park.

Stigmata

My jester. My boy. How you fill up the world.

Your tattoos are a vista of splats and squirts,

tapping into an abstract realm that is

your only true home.

The sweat of your labors

flinging in beads and pellets onto bar patrons

christens them in the name of all that is holy.

Fingers digging holes into guitar necks,

strings scraping like

sandpaper against frets,

erosion re-contouring sound.

Limbs a full string section

tremolo'ing in dramatic suspense.

Singing voice an otherworldly spillage of

grade C maple syrup, silky, dark and dense.

Your grunge. Anthemic. Stigmatic.

The American flag is draped over

empty caskets at your blood-spurting

defiance, your insistence on life and living.

Hell, boy, you don't need a damned kidney.

A damned kidney needs you.

The Administering of the Medicine

That his new wife is willing to shave

the top of his head for him,

leaving alone the sides and back

(classic "C-haircut" of men with

male-patterned baldness), just

so he can throw on his See's Candies

employee shirt, some Fred Mertz

pants belted at the boobs,

Instagram it, and get an uncontainable

laughter from his family, who are a

family that loves to laugh, and

laughs infectiously, eternal children,

each one, tells me that he picked

the right woman to marry,

and that she intimately

understands the protocol.

The Antigens No One Was Looking For

In all the many blood draws taken for the tissue typing and cross-matching, could any of those tests have ever portended these compatibilities?

Who else could I give a book of Dali's paintings *and* vintage LPs of Parliament Funkadelic *and* a Bukowski poem to, and have their head explode out of sympatico? All culled from my 30-year-old collections, and dusty with your DNA before you were even given to this earth.

Who else could make an animated short of the two of us tossing Virgil around (V the kidney), with cartoon blood dripping from both our guts, and chipmunk-sounding laughter, and knowing instinctively that I would find that funny?

Who else, out of a hundred people in a room, all dancing and crunking to a Ludacris cut at my father's 80th birthday party, could stumble upon Dad's painting entitled "Agony" and stop stunned, responding to an ancestral tug of some vague but pertinent nature that would always connect us through pain, and deliverance, and pain again?

we adjust the volume and tweak the contrast

Between Skin and Bone

I lost my left nipple in a surgery that went wrong.

Now I constantly finger the scar that has taken its place.

I could probably get a job in fetish porn.

I lost my left kidney in a surgery that went right.

Now I constantly finger the 4 laparoscopic dots on the left

side of my stomach that have formed a horseshoe

that changes shape every time I gain-&-lose 20 pounds.

I am a map of scars, a highland landscape of corporeal Braille

that my curious index finger cannot seem to leave alone. There

are days when I wear the scars like trophies, but far more days

when I plot my next tatts to camouflage them. Purists of the form

scoff at the idea of hiding one's bodily imperfections with a

tattoo: "Ink for expression's sake, not from shame."

I got my first tatt shortly after the transplant. Marking the triumph.

It's a beautifully detailed Marquesan-style tribal that is

gradually crawling up the left arm.

Everything in my life seems to occur on the left.

Hans followed his first-ever shortly after me, but has, by now,

far surpassed me in the Great Tattoo Race, as he navigates

the precarious terrain of morbidity and survival

from the newly rejecting organ, and

I am just trying to love my flesh somehow.

Between skin and bone there lies a hint of where we come from,

and who emerges to take on this life. We gather our pieces

and build from there. We adjust the volume and tweak the

contrast. Sometimes we baptize it with ink. We sully our knees

to find support from the cosmos, and outstretch our hands

to make connection. And we breathe.

As plot would have it, not a single one of my tatts touches

any of my scars. Turns out the purists might actually

have something there. I seem to have grown quite in love

with this hypertrophic body art of mine, born not from

a desire to express myself in ink, but out of a handful of dirty

dogfights for somebody's right to keep breathing.

The Myth of Tacrolimus

You titled

one of

your songs

after your

anti-rejection

drugs.

An unwieldy

unpronounceable

thing

that

reminisces

of a

Roman

god.

Then

proceeded

to compose

the most

hair-raising

elegy to

rejection

in all its

divisive

forms

that has

ever

curdled

my

blood.

In that

Instant

I knew the

depth of you.

Lift

We've never much talked about the renal trauma
you experienced at birth because the cord tangled
around your infant neck. That time we interviewed
with a local radio station, and you told the story with

me sitting next to you, I kept nodding my head as
you told it, pretending I knew more of the story than
I did, because it suddenly hit me that I've never much
asked you about these things. And the one lesson I

was supposed to learn from this odyssey was less
self-absorption, yet here I was, learning details about
it for the first time, while being caught on camera,
and just doing my best to act as if I knew more, and

kicking myself for not actually knowing more. We've
never much talked about what it feels like to have a
sentence thrown down at birth like that. Entering this
world with the hardwiring of strangulation already in

place. How could you know it isn't supposed to be that way? And because all the ways in which one is an artist does stave off death awhile, I wonder if you became an artist because you instinctively knew that, or if artist

was destined to be your story no matter the rest. And now that you are in need of a saving grace yet again, we've talked very little, though I have no problem bombarding people on Facebook. I really want to tell

you that I have largely kept out of it because I see your pain and don't wish to drum up more. But I think we both know that what we're actually dealing with here is a heavy, lumbering vat of my excuses, toppled over

by cowardice, content spilling and spreading across the floor like sewage. Lift your feet before it touches your toes and soaks the dye of my fears deeply into your skin. Do not allow my nonsense to stain you.

Lift.

Pondering Black

Black is the color of my hair, or was, before the melanin stopped infusing my strands, and the white wisps began giving me away.

Black is the clothing of my preference (slimming, for starters) when many have wondered if the penchant doesn't signal something worrisome.

Black is the race you started checking off on all of your medical forms after the transplant, though you have a German mother and a Mexican father, because you are silly. But also because you are brave enough to disarm it. And your silliness did not diminish with the infusion of Virgil-the-Kidney's more humorless cells, thank god, and I prefer you silly because now that you are down again, for but a minute, silly is what will see you through.

Black is the simplistic symbol of evil that archetypal lore has divined, where white is pure, and gray the unknown that frightens us even more.

Black is the heroic and the good reclaimed by those
of us decidedly reframing lore.

Black is the cave Joseph Campbell tells me is the key
to my redemption. My prize in this life, if I'm willing to
seek it out, climb in there, face the beast, and claim it.

Black is the hole out of which I cannot seem to climb for any
satisfactory length of time. And there is no past tense for that
sentence. It lives in the constantly rounding feedback of rising
and sinking, and whatever tools I can gather for managing it.

Black is the gleaming chess piece I'll play and play, vicious
gamesman that I am, till my queen is toppled into the black night.

Black is the night that brilliances the stars that foretold a young
man whose life needed saving. And who saved a life in return.

Black is the lights-out that is not yet yours, my boy.
Turn and walk the other way now.

Love Letter to His New Donor (a summoner's aubade)

Dearest friend,

May I call you this? We'll soon both be

members of a cherished club,

and as such I feel, already, a kinship.

As I write this, the mouths of the

purple morning-glories beyond my window

are achingly gaped,

singing your praises I like to think,

knowing you are coming,

and the sun is brilliant, almost white,

on this late-winter morning

after a week of sunless rain.

You are coming. This I know.

And I feel hope, which scares me some.

I ask only this:

Walk deliberately toward it.

Trip and fall, if it comes to it, but take no prisoners, least of all him.

Expose panties. Jump back up. Make a joke out of the spill,

scrappy like I know you must be.

Then keep on stepping high.

Keep him in gentle accord.

Keep yourself there too.

Above all, breathe. The dark nights for both of you

will soften their edges, and the morning-glory

will yawn again each dawn to remind you that you are *AS* glorious.

Send me a postcard from beyond the moon.

I hung out there myself once.

We'll regale together this love supreme that

keeps us all rallying for one another.

While Eating Lunch In the Neighborhood and Listening to His Newest CD

It's clear he's having a blast.

Twisting our brains with abstract-expressionist lyrics

that take a second, third, or even tenth

listen to fully decode. And like any one

of the most gut-twisting canvases of de Kooning

or Basquiat, it doesn't really matter if we ever do.

It's also clear there's pain.

His music, both operatic *and* romping in the playground of

electronic innovations, seems to be telling a singular story. That of death.

Ordinarily such a heaviness of theme coming from a young man would give

me pause, and great discomfort. But I know where he's been.

I know the beast he wrestles daily.

As the waitress approaches

and prompts me to remove my ear buds and let her know

if I need another refill on my iced tea, I turn to her, pulse racing:

"You know what? Damn. If our pain can't be recast into song,

if it can't be funneled into something that shifts us where we stand,

if it can't issue us a new pair of eyes,

then what is this whole plot twist for?"

I hand her my ear buds.

Postscript

Viscera released on December 29, 2019.
On August 29, 2020, Hans San Juan successfully received his second kidney transplant.

#donatelife
#shareyourspare

Angela Carole Brown is the recipient of the North Street Book Prize in literary fiction for her novel *Trading Fours*, and the SoulWord Magazine Poetry Prize for her poem "Cotton Candy." She is also the author of the novel *The Assassination of Gabriel Champion*, the poetry collection *Bones*, and the 100-word story collection *Aleatory on the Radio*. She writes the blog Bindi Girl Chronicles. She has also been on the L.A. music scene for over three decades as a singer, songwriter, and recording artist, has produced several albums of music in the genres of jazz and folk, and is the lead singer in Elvis Schoenberg's Orchestre Surreal. She is featured in the documentary film *The Goddess Project*. In 2008, Angela donated a kidney to Hans San Juan, which has been recounted in her memoir *The Kidney Journals: Memoirs of a Desperate Lifesaver*. *Viscera* marks her first poetry chapbook.

www.angelacarolebrown.com
www.bit.ly/BooksByAngelaCaroleBrown
Facebook @angelacarolebrown
Instagram @bindigirlchronicles
Twitter @angelacarolebro